Insects All Around

by Margie Burton, Cathy French, and Tammy Jones

Table of Contents

What Is an Insect?

An insect has
six legs and
three body parts.

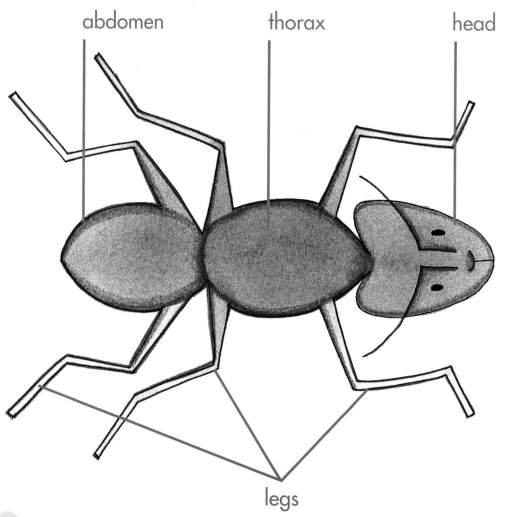

abdomen   thorax   head

legs

These are all insects.

Butterfly

Mosquito

Beetle

Ants

What Does an Insect Look Like?

Many insects are very, very small. They are not even one inch long.

The smallest insects can go through the hole in this needle.

Some insects are big.

Rhinoceros Beetle

Some insects are more than four inches long.

Many insects have antennae.
They use them to smell
and feel.

Cockroach

Many insects have
two eyes.
They cannot move
their eyes or see
very far. Their eyes
stay open all of the time.

Fly

Dragonfly

Some insects make sounds.

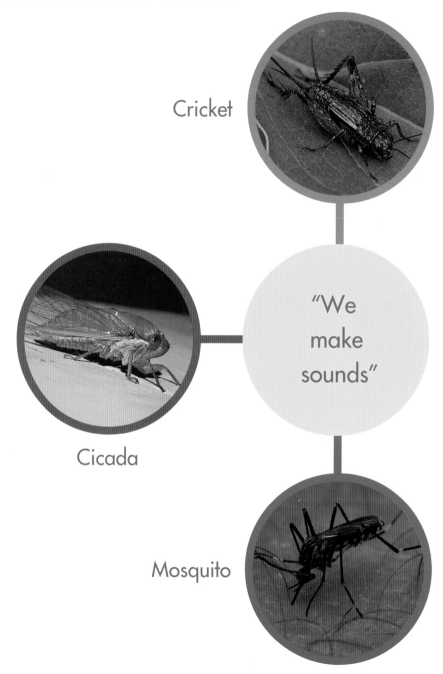

Cricket

Cicada

"We make sounds"

Mosquito

Many insects can hide.
Can you see the insects?

This insect looks
like a stick.

Walking Stick

This insect looks
like a green leaf.

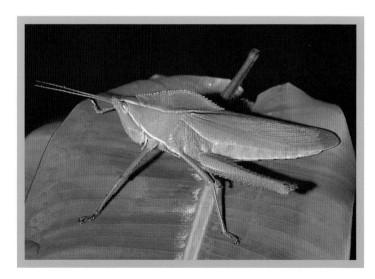

Grasshopper

What Can Insects Do?

Some insects can fly.

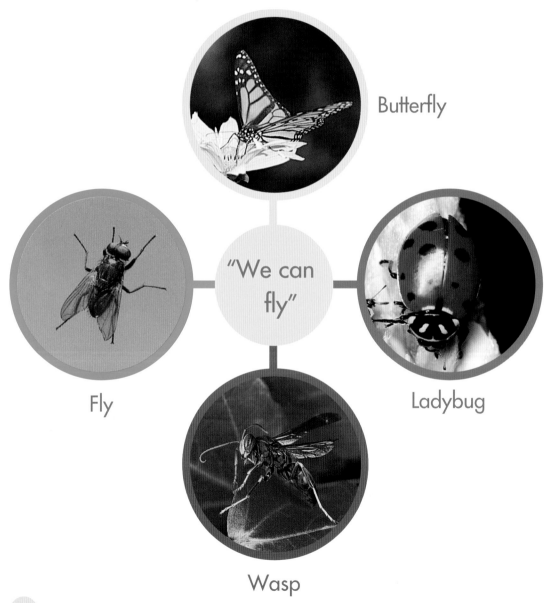

Butterfly

"We can fly"

Fly

Ladybug

Wasp

Insects fly so that they
can look for food.
They also fly
so that they can
get away from animals.

Lizards eat insects.

Many animals eat insects.

Birds eat insects.

Frogs eat insects, too.

How Can Insects Help?

Some insects can help the plants make seeds. Bees go from plant to plant getting sweet food. When they do this, they help to make new seeds.

Bee

Bees also give us honey.

They take
the sweet food
back to
the hive and
make the honey.

How Can Insects Be Pests?

Some insects eat plants.

Beetles eat leaves.

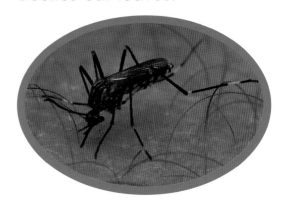

Some insects bite us.

Mosquitos bite us.

Some insects hurt
our homes.

Termites hurt our homes.

Insects are all around us.